THE
HEART'S
CURTAIN

Also by Madeleine Onraet

Minjerribah

THE
HEART'S CURTAIN

poems

MADELEINE ONRAET

Insight Poetry

First published in 2022 by Insight Poetry

Copyright © Madeleine Onraet 2022
Visit: www.madeleineonraet.com

All rights reserved.

No part of this publication may be reproduced, stored in a retrieval system, or transmitted, in any form or by any means, electronic, mechanical, photocopying, recording or otherwise without the prior written permission of the publisher.

Excerpt from poem by Rumi translated by Hamid Homayouni

Cover design by Jelena Mirkovic

ISBN (paperback) 978-0-6453474-2-5
ISBN (ebook) 978-0-6453474-3-2

For Jean and Anne

Contents

Introduction 1

The Heart's Curtain

Path 5
Question 7
Open 9
Explorer 11
Remember 13
Don't go 15
Gobble 17
Bite 19
Apprentice 21
Quest 23
Sky fields 25
Shadows 27
The heart's curtain 29
Art gallery café 31
Exposed 33
Point 35
It is our shallowness 37
Chrysalis 39

Calling 41
Light 43
Core 45
Centre 47
Rain falls on the horizon's edge 49
Welcome 51
Mirror 53
E-*go* 55
Wound 57
Wings 59

Through the Window

Tears must fall 63
Memo from the path 65
A summer's day 67
If you can be kind 69
Marketplace 71
Busy 73
Excavating 75
Intrinsic 77
Walking meditation 79
What is my body 81
Empty vessel 83
Unforeseen 85
Tender 87

FALLING STAR   89
PRAYER   91
NIGHT SKY   93
LIFE PRACTICE   95
DISSOLVE   97
PRODIGAL   99
A CHRISTMAS   101
INTIMATE   103
TIDAL   105
SATURDAY   107
UNEXPECTED   109
HERMITAGE   111
FAMILY EXPRESS   113
FOSSICKING   115
LENTEN   117
HOUSEHOLDER   119
GLISTENING   121
IN STORMS OF MIND   123
SPRING GARDEN   125
ALIGNMENT   127
BOUNDLESS   129
UNVEILED   131

Acknowledgments   133
About the author   135

Your pains are messengers
Listen to them.

- Rumi

Introduction

These poems are insights that emerged on a spiritual path, a journey to know who and what I am, and what is the nature of suffering in life.

I offer these poems to those wanting to know themselves more deeply. To live is to encounter suffering, but how we respond to suffering impacts the direction and happiness of our life and those around us.

These poems emerged over a decade as insights arising from inquiry into my immediate direct experience. During this period, I practised journal writing every morning as part of my daily life, raising two sons with my husband and contributing to the wellbeing of our local community.

I discovered suffering to be a potential portal to depth, and that in our depth, there is the peace that comes from understanding who we truly are. Our hearts become strong, our minds capable instruments of wisdom.

When we reflect and listen deeply, we can learn the meaning of love and what it is to be human, which is to be kind and fully present to ourselves and others as a loving light in this world.

The Heart's Curtain

Path

Love
woke her
with a kiss
and said:
Be mine.

Truth
tore down
her door
and blew
her mind.

Compassion
came with
sweet mint balm
to hold the world.

And all because
she dared to
walk
a
path.

Question

Who am I?

I have found it
simplest
to begin

with everything
I'm not.

Open

When I allow
the space
in the tightness
of a day

and I allow
the breath,
I enter God.

The error
is not
so much
our busyness.

It is our strange
refusal
to allow.

Explorer

We have such need
to climb
into the darkness
of ourselves.

How else
are we to learn
what it is
our hearts
most seek?

Stars form
in the arms
of deep
space.

Remember

The earth is your friend
and the body
does not lie.
Whatever is
your deepest need,
sit with trees.
Spread the loveliness
of your own soul
and find the blossom
of your heart;
its quiet majesty
awaits your return.
An end
to this strange neglect
of you.

Don't go

You know
that way you check
ahead of time

for what's not
really there,
yet could eventuate
(but rarely does).

If you saw
how many times
you'd left the room

before the bliss
could reach
your waiting heart,
you'd weep.

Gobble

Greed and
gluttony
reside
in gobble.

Twist
my understanding
of a sweet
treat

into more and more and more
refusing to feel

what's
here
now
within.

Bite

When the harshest bite
comes from someone close,
we gasp.
For then we cannot
so easily divide
against it.

The darkness is close,
so close
it manifests
the hidden
places
of our pride,
laid bare for us
to weep.

Apprentice

Do not let anyone
lay false responsibility
upon you in your heart

nor clothe you
with the weight
of their own cowardice
concealed as victimhood.

Until you are master,
you cannot properly
carry these.

Impeccability
is being truly with
life
as it is.

The task now
is to deeply learn,
to be.

Quest

In the room you fear
you'll find your courage.

It waits for you
beneath the seat
of staying with.

God asks nothing
that God will not send;
the something
that you need.

It's all a wild adventuring,

precisely yours

to live.

Sky fields

Like a bird,
my heart
wants to sing.

Does the bird
ask: Can I?
The bird just sings.

Back off, doubt.

And now
there is the Quiet.

Always there is love –
Singing.

Shadows

Fear hides
in the thickets
of the mind.

Fear feigns
elusiveness
and sleight
of hand.

Once sighted,
once caught,
it weakens.

That steady and
relentless
gaze –
Love's needed
penetration.

Courage
rising
from the seat
of clear light.

The heart's curtain

Behind the heart's
curtain
and the mind's
door,
there is such pain.

We need to sit awhile,
like this.

We need to sit awhile
in Kindness.

Art gallery café

So often, our harshest voice
is towards ourselves.
Why do we
perpetuate destruction
of the good?
We would not tolerate it
out there
yet we permit it within.

Sitting here beneath a balm of trees,
their orange leaves
the feathers of a bird's wing
opening vitality –
a heart's wish to live
as succulence,
free.

I cannot change events
that led to a development
in me of darkness.
Yet I can demand respect
in me for everything I find.
Cruelty only has its way
when life is narrowed
to a flimsy definition of itself.

Exposed

It is the intensity
of a heart
stripped,
vulnerable –
that's where we
learn to live
what courage is.

Point

A theology degree
is earned
in the substance
of my life.

What point is
a piece of paper
pinned
to a wall

if I have not learned
how to die.

It is our shallowness
that tortures us.

Chrysalis

Hurt collapses
Pain aches
Judgment bludgeons.

But the heart
is big enough
for these.

Love forms
wings –
emerges as Peace.

Calling

It seems to me
that just a day
lived in honesty

as to what you
really feel about
everything you usually do

without considering
why you do them
or how

would be enough
to throw your life
heart first
into your destiny.

Light

I am standing
in the kitchen
thinking

when I become
aware...
sunlight

on my skin
is warm.
Pear

in my mouth
is sweet.
It's simple.

We just
continually
forget.

Core

One day, after years
of intense exploration,
I decided I would not
be so brutally cruel
to myself
and refused
the inner critic.

I gave my full attention
to the family
food shop
and baked a cake
for the school raffle.

The shift was subtle
yet radical.

When we get right down
into the core of it,
it's clear.

It can just take years
of ancestral daze
to appear.

Centre

There are painters
sanding outside
walls. And a son
upstairs has tv on.
And a son downstairs
blasts rock.
And I am here
hearing it all
as I sense the Quiet.
Feel it rising
through my body
as deliciousness,
as Smile.

Rain falls on the horizon's edge

yet here is still.
I reach my hand
into the dream,
sense the quiet
on a bent
knee
of cloud,
and pray –
everything I ask
will be reborn
as gratitude.
Every light
will make its
way into my heart.

Welcome

Every confessional
needs a sign
above its door
saying: Welcome.

Everything we are
is received.
And if a priest
tells you otherwise,
forgive him.

He has momentarily
forgotten
Love's want
of us.

Mirror

A heart's rest is in its offering.
We want –
then find the deeper pleasure
is to give.

We hurt –
then sense the heart's expansion
towards the one who
hurt.

The mind might not always
understand the heart's ways,
but it will recognise
the flooding of peace

that heart's wisdom brings.
It is inevitable,
being Kindness.

E-*GO*

I seek.
I seek and seek and seek
to find
I've failed.

Yet to weep
in full
and devastating
knowledge
of my failure

is beginning
to be ready
when Love comes –
as Emptying.

Wound

It is strange to walk and talk,
appearing normal
to the people you meet
in the superficial realms,
when you know
you walk as wound.

Its walls are an exquisite sensitivity
of hurt
you have feared
with every fibre of yourself,
a place you thought
was death.

Now you have been given strength
to turn towards
what's here,
you find a bruised
bloodied tissue of the soul.

You walk within the wound
and find not death
but human dignity.
Inside the horribleness,
not end
but understanding.

Who you truly are
is deeper than this
and the wound
a portal into Vast.

Wound is home.
A wisdom you can speak
into eternity –
your Awe hushed as breath.

Wings

Love wants us.
Our want is Love.
And the journey
will release
the butterflies
held in glass jars
within your heart
for so long.

Their beauty
will astound you.

Through the Window

Tears must fall

I understand
I am enough.
That people are vulnerable
whoever they are.
And yes, brutality exists.
And cruelty.

Ignorance is ours
to know
and weep over. Till we are sure
in the telling and through
all the tears,
we are
and have always been
enough.

Memo from the path

We think the suffering will go.
It doesn't.

We think confusion ends.
Still here.

What happens is we begin
to see through it.

We begin to know it
for what it is.

A summer's day

I popped up
as if through a hole
in the ground
into an open

sunny field.

No one here
but a simplicity,
a sun-splashed warmth

of heart.

If you can be kind,
be kind.

It is your destiny.

Marketplace

When Truth kicks out the legs
of the last pedestal you have
been sold for.

When there is no one left
to use deceit to blind you
to the dignity of your own self.

When lies sold as wishing wells
can swallow you no longer,
you'll have quietly arrived.

You'll be dangerous now,
for you'll be wise
and unafraid of your aloneness.

Busy

Underneath
your haste,
your lists,
trying to fix,
to get it done,
your continual
catching up.

Underneath
all this
there is your life,
waiting.

Excavating

We might continually
avoid our pain
but deep within
we're terrified
of happiness.

Intrinsic

It is the light in you
I see.

Within the gloom,
the inadequacy
and stark
despair.

It is the radiance in you
I see –
and
I believe.

Walking Meditation

In morning walking,
earth tells me
of her kindness.

I feel it rising
as a revelation born
of my receptiveness.

An Indigenous man
said recently
after his dance,
"It's all right here,
you know,
in your back yard."

And I am Here.
And he is right.

What is my body
but a beacon
of You.

Empty vessel

It's noble –
this art

of serving
family.

Simply
Being.

Unforeseen

Forgiveness is power.

We are divested
of the burden
of revenge
and there is peace.

In our depths,
forgiveness chooses us
when we are ready.

Tender

I do not feel I can so easily
go out
today.

Love's taking me.

Falling star

If I had not been rejected,
I might not have incubated
in the necessary solitude.

If I had not failed,
I might not
have opened.

We cannot know
when we will meet Truth
as a Way.

We feel it – and in
feeling fully,
we know.

Prayer

Prayer began to find me.
To emerge through me so
I was nothing but this prayer.

We do not then say our prayers.
Eventually our prayers say us.
(And always did.)

Night sky

We think we know
what we want,
but life has other plans.

Life practice

Morning walking can be offering.
As can pegging clothes.
Ironing
(remarkably!).
And sweeping paving stones in
the late afternoon.

Everything can bear the light
of gratitude
with an open heart.

Dissolve

One can walk from sweetness
round a corner
into meanness.

Love can so easily
twist
as hate.

And resolution
disappears as fast
as it appeared.

Passing into wakefulness,
the eye
can blink

until the heart reveals
the steadiness
we need.

There's nothing that the
Deep Heart
cannot receive.

Prodigal

Stubborn
sits
apart.

Till stubborn
understands
it, too, is welcome.

Even stubborn
melts in Joy
in being known.

A Christmas

When forgiveness came,
we were indeed gathered
in a small room,
but instead of tongues
of fire and great gusts,
it came upon us quietly
and subtly as the sound
of juniper releasing oil
in a palm.

I felt its lubricating love,
beginning with myself
and extending to include
everyone.

Forgiveness glides
like elder swans at dusk
for it has that deepest power
of settling us
in peace.

We no longer have the need
for words,
nor to know
flight.

Intimate

Walking beneath the trees
I feel You,
a presence in the air
pressing through my clothes
and down my legs
and breathed
through my toes.

Walking beneath the trees
I feel You,
a Potency
breathing me
alive.

Tidal

To allow the disappointment
as a wave,
to take you to the stark shores
of nothingness
without the stagnancy of gloom
or bitterness,
is a maturity
hard-won.

We feel the waves
again
and again
until the shore
appears.

Everything we seek
waits
within.

Saturday

Cleaning house can feel like a prayer
or an intense irritation.

Both please God –
where there's sincerity.

Unexpected

Woken in the night
by silence,
then the sudden
sound
of rain

ravishes me.
God's
like that!

Hermitage

I read online of a
hermit nun
who said she returns
to solitude
and to silence
the way most
people
return to
family.

I return each day
to family
in the silence
and the solitude of
who
I truly
am.

Family express

A day can become so full of noise,
the scattering of dice
thrown into mayhem.

Yet a breath
taken with full consciousness
of nothing but the breath

brings me to You
like a child's return
to Mother.

Fossicking

May my life
serve Truth
in its tiny, most
insignificant
moments.

Here, where my
preferences
conceal You,
Thy Will be done.

LENTEN

After laughing till I cry
at a Lenten family meal:
"I want to be a laughing
saint," I say. "It's not
further crucifixion that
we need. It's Joy."

Householder

After days of loss of You

I find You
in these moments
of my sacrifice

driving through the night
into the rain,
hearing songs

play on the radio.
Softness
melting my heart

absorbed

in

Beauty.

Glistening

First light –
it is the sight
of a water
drop

upon a leaf.

And later in the day,
in the scramble
of a house
playing blame
games,

it is the innocence
of rain
falling on the
garden

that transmutes me –

the way
Christ
asks.

In storms of mind,
sensing the body
brings me Home.

Spring garden

Morning stillness
has, this afternoon,
become a breeze
and sun is warm.

I'm always
leaning through
a window
into You, like a child
will constantly
return
to know a mother's heart;
we peer through what is seen
with an assuredness.

The invisible impresses most.

Curled like a shyness
round her one
love,
forget-me-nots
of clasping,

while a soul yearns
and birds
so effortlessly wing
within my hopefulness,
my leap of soul –
towards You.

Alignment

I hear
at crucial
moments:

Will you die?

I hear
and turn,
with Yes.

Boundless

An adversary
of my early life
taught me this.
We can be wrong
while sure of right
and yet be right
nevertheless.
For like a plant
burgeoning
as revelation
on a green stem
of growth,
we understand
at some worthy
stage
life is not ours
to direct.
It has its own
accord and mantra
we may one day
fall into.

And when we do,
whatever we do,
however we do it,

we'll know
it is not ours,
it's Love's.

Unveiled

I cannot take
away
your pain.

But I can tell you
pain
need not have
the last
word.

I can tell you
Truth has that.

And at the heart
of Truth

is
Peace.

Acknowledgments

My thanks to the students and teachers of the Diamond Approach Australia community. Your love of the truth is a flame. My appreciation to the parish community of Saints Peter and Paul, Bulimba. Your daily service is a light on the hill. To my husband, Steve, my gratitude for your love and encouragement.

About the Author

Madeleine Onraet writes poetry that focuses on the spiritual nature of existence, family life and the natural world. Raised a Catholic, Madeleine has explored the wisdom and beauty of mystical Christianity and has been a student of the Diamond Approach since 2002. She has worked as a print journalist and hospital chaplain. Madeleine lives in Brisbane with her husband, Steve. They are blessed with two sons.

www.ingramcontent.com/pod-product-compliance
Lightning Source LLC
Chambersburg PA
CBHW020324010526
44107CB00054B/1975